# ED EMBERLEY'S
# FINGERPRINT
## Drawing Book

LITTLE, BROWN & COMPANY

LB kids™
NEW YORK BOSTON
lb-kids.com

This book shows how to make pictures using your fingerprints and a few scribbles, dots, and lines....

This row shows what to draw. ← This row shows where to put it.

Simple step-by-step instructions show you how.

1. Press ink.   2. Press paper.   3. Draw.

# ABOUT PRINTERS

Your finger will do for a start.

For cleaner hands and a greater choice of sizes you can make your own stampers.

An artist's gum-rubber eraser is easy to carve and fun to use.

So are assorted veggies such as carrots or potatoes.

For a very special gift, for yourself or someone else, you can have a custom rubber stamp made from your fingerprint. Inquire at any printer or office-supply store.

# ABOUT INK PADS

There are a number of different kinds of ink pads you can use. Office stamp pads are inexpensive and can be found in places that sell office supplies. Colors are limited to red, blue, black, and sometimes green.

CAUTION: Since pads are made for adult office use, the ink is not necessarily nontoxic or washable.

Craft stamp pads are harder to find and usually more expensive than standard office ink pads. They can be found in many places that sell arts and crafts supplies. They come in lots of bright colors and are available washable and nontoxic.

You could also try making your own ink pads from cloth or paper towels and whatever coloring you have on hand. This is the least expensive way to go, but it will take some experimentation to get just the right combination of paint and pad.

Of course, you are not limited to stamping or printing. Cut paper, fabric, stencils, blobs of paint, lumps of clay—anything with which you can make a roundish shape will work using these instructions.

# ABOUT MARKERS

A pencil will do for a start.

After that, which marker you choose will depend on the size of your print and the ink used.

For this book I used a colored pencil for the colored lines and a fine-point fiber-tip pen for the black lines. Both were found in the stationery section of my local drugstore.

## ODDS AND ENDS

You will also need paper to print on and a table to work on; plastic or newspapers to protect the table; work clothes to protect the artist; and paper towels and soap and water for cleaning up.

There are billions of fingerprints in the world.
No two have ever been found that are just alike.
There never has been and there never will be fingerprints just like yours.
That makes your fingerprints very special.

## THIS AND THAT
### CIRCLES AND OVALS

I used two kinds of fingerprints to make this book. Ovals and circles.

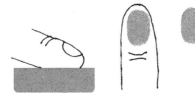

The ovals were made by using my whole fingertip.

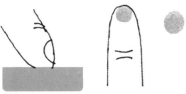

The circles were made by using just the very tip of my finger.

For carrot printing, use a straight cut for circles, and an angled cut for ovals.

Adult supervision is advised for ALL cutting.

### ONE OR MANY

Sometimes when I make fingerprint pictures, I like to use just one color at a time because it's quick and easy.

Sometimes I use lots of colors and lots of fingers.

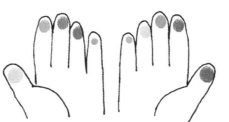

When I want to change colors, I dip my finger in a glass of water and then wipe it off on a stack of paper towels. That keeps my ink pads bright and clean.

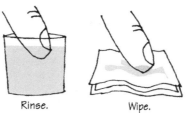

Rinse.          Wipe.

## EXTRA FOR EXPERTS
### HALF PRINTS

In a few places in this book, I used half prints. Here's how I made them.

1. Place paper shield.
2. Print half on, half off paper shield.
3. Remove paper shield.
4. Draw.

1. Print.
2. Cover with paper shield.
3. Print half on, half off paper shield.

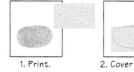

4. Remove paper shield.
5. Draw.
Too complicated? Use just one color.

Half circles are just right for making watermelons, monkeys, and other things. Can you find the half prints in these two things?

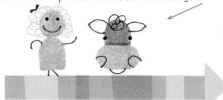

# THE GARDEN

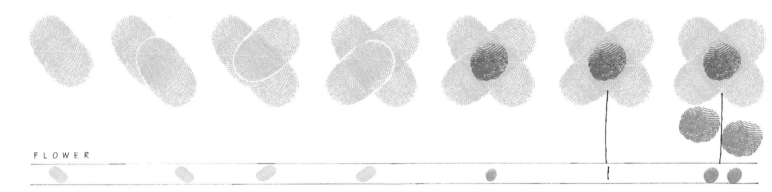

FLOWER

SNAIL .

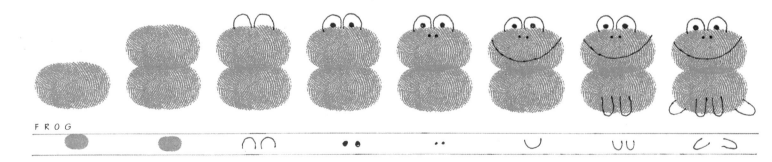

FROG

4

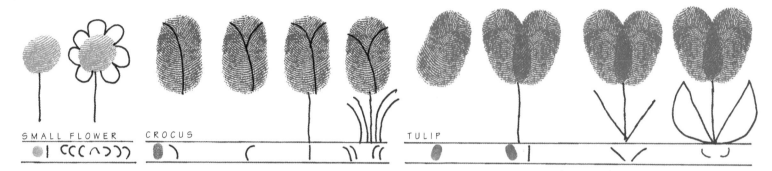

SMALL FLOWER

CROCUS

TULIP

BROWN ANT

CATERPILLAR

CENTIPEDE

BUMBLEBEE

# THE POND

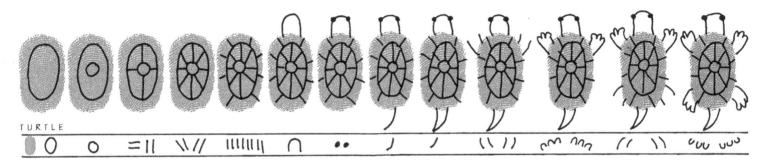

TURTLE

DUCK

POLLYWOG

BUTTERFLY

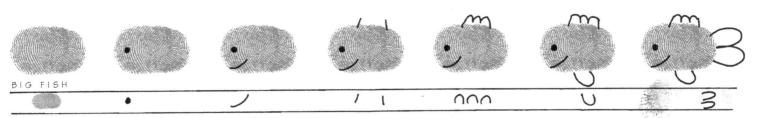

SWIMMING FROG

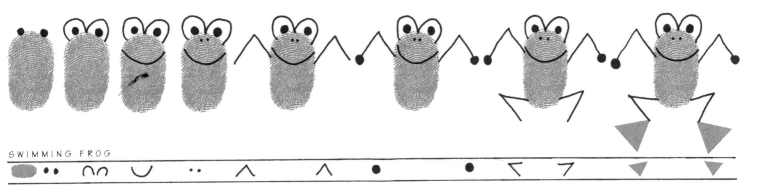

BIG FISH

LITTLE FISH

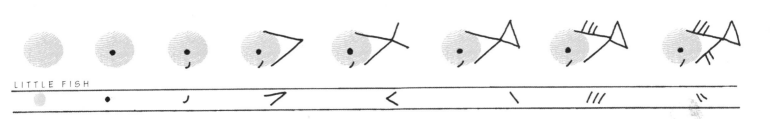

7

# FINGERLINGS

I ALSO CALL THESE MY
TEENY TINIES. I USE A
DIFFERENT FINGERTIP FOR
EACH COLOR.

SPRING

SUMMER

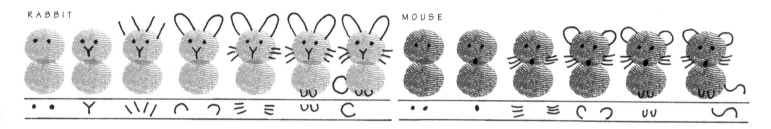

RABBIT

MOUSE

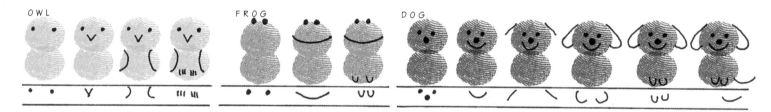

OWL

FROG

DOG

BEAVER

FALL     FALL     WINTER

SITTING CAT

BIRD

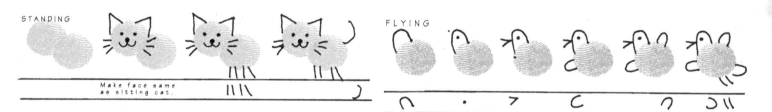

STANDING

Make face same
as sitting cat.

FLYING

RUNNING

Make face same
as sitting cat.

PECKING

# ANIMALS

ELEPHANT

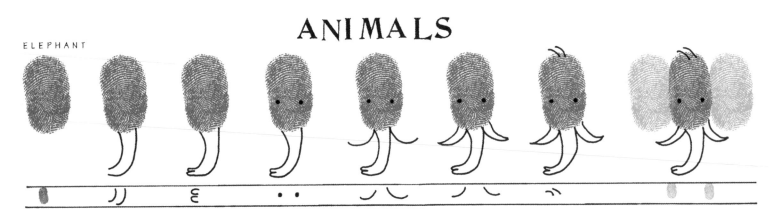

BABY ELEPHANT

LION

10

**BABY MONKEY**

**MONKEY**

**ALLIGATOR**

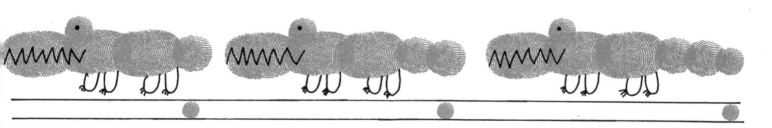

# MORE ANIMALS

RACCOON

PIG

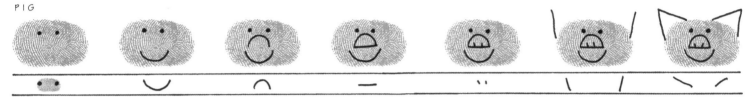

BEAVER

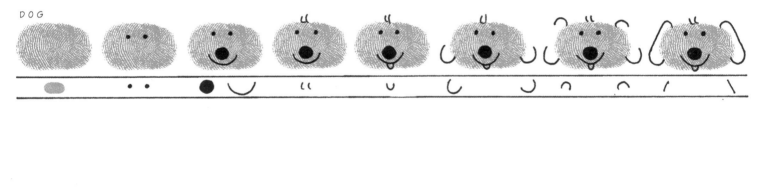

DOG

CAT

SMALL BULLDOG

MOUSE

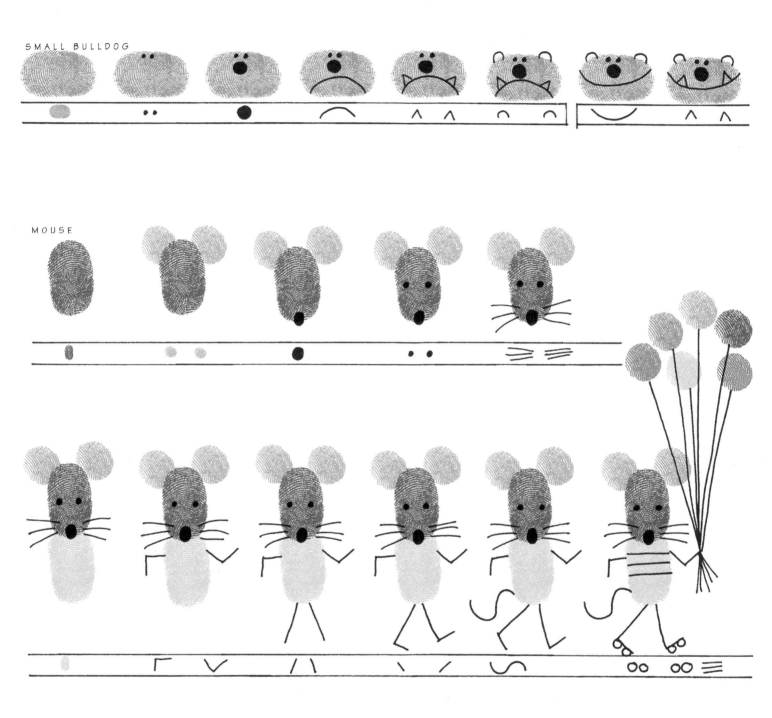

BIG BULLDOG

# BIRDS

BABY BIRDS IN NEST

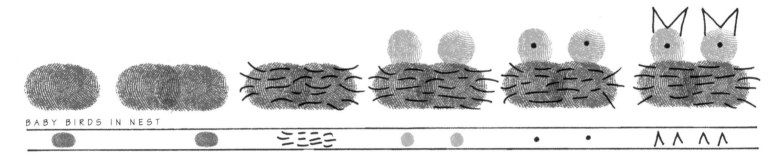

BIRD EATING WORM

BIRD FRONT VIEW

BIRD BACK VIEW

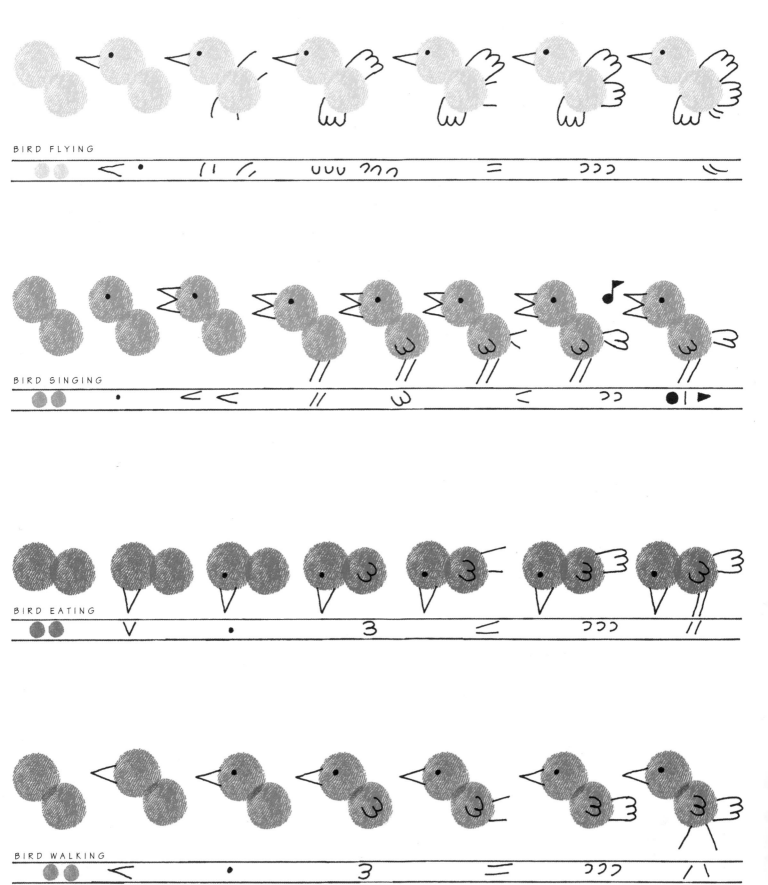

BIRD FLYING

BIRD SINGING

BIRD EATING

BIRD WALKING

# BEAN BUDDIES

I THINK FINGERPRINTS LOOK LIKE LITTLE BEANS. I LIKE TO USE THESE LITTLE "FINGER BEANS" TO MAKE ALL DIFFERENT KINDS OF LITTLE BEAN BUDDIES.

BASIC

PEA BEAN BUDDY　　BAKED BEAN BUDDY　　LIMA BEAN BUDDY　　JELLY BEAN BUDDY

SPEAKING

POINTING

YAWNING

CELEBRATING

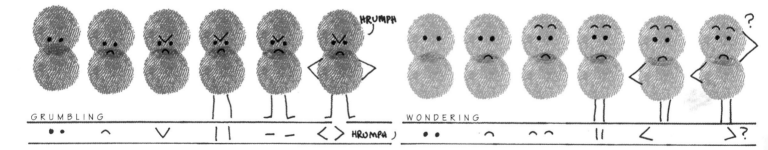

GRUMBLING

WONDERING

16

WALKING

JOGGING

RUNNING

WINNING

BALLET

HULA

CLOG
DANCING

TAP DANCING

LITTLE CLOWN

NAPOLEON

SAILOR

QUEEN    KING    PRINCE

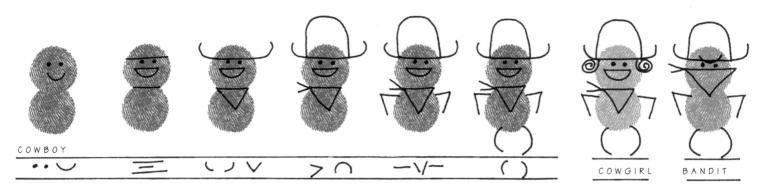

COWBOY

COWGIRL    BANDIT

PIRATE

SUPERPERSON

EVIL VILLAIN

# FEELINGS

HAPPY  VERY HAPPY  VERY VERY HAPPY  SNOOTY

SAD  VERY SAD  VERY VERY SAD

UPSET  ANGRY  VERY ANGRY  VERY VERY ANGRY

SLY (MISCHIEVOUS)  SHY (EMBARRASSED)  SUSPICIOUS  HURTING

OUCH!
OUCH!

MUSIC  HUMMING  MMM  WHISTLING  SINGING  SINGERS

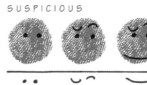

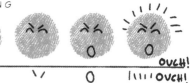

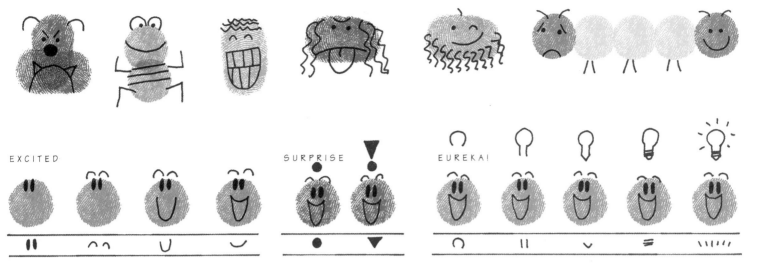

EXCITED

SURPRISE

EUREKA!

PUZZLED

IN LOVE

BOP!

SLEEPY

ASLEEP

SNORING

SICK

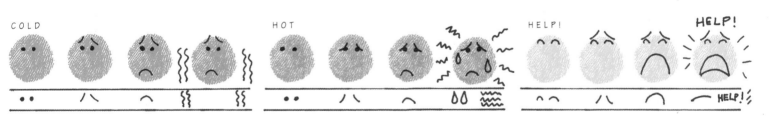

COLD

HOT

HELP!

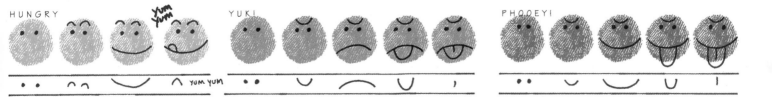

HUNGRY

YUM YUM

YUKI

PHOOEY!

SKIPPING ROPE

BICYCLING

SKATEBOARDING

ROLLER-SKATING

22

APRIL SHOWERS

FISHING

HIKING

KITES

# SUMMER FUN

CHASING BUTTERFLIES

SWIMMING

SURFING

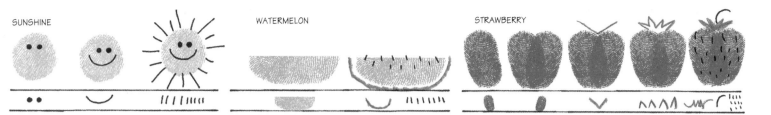

SUNSHINE

WATERMELON

STRAWBERRY

LAWN MOWING

SUNBATHING

BASEBALL

# FALL FUN

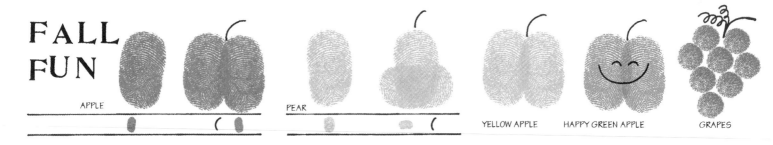

APPLE

PEAR

YELLOW APPLE   HAPPY GREEN APPLE

GRAPES

FARMING

LACROSSE

SOCCER

FOOTBALL

SPORTS FAN

CHEERLEADER

BASKETBALL

# WINTER FUN

PENGUIN FRONT VIEW

PENGUIN SIDE VIEW

SNOWPERSON

**SKIING**

**SKATING**

**HOCKEY**

# HOLIDAYS

EASTER BUNNY

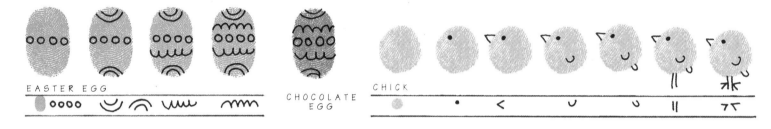

EASTER EGG

CHOCOLATE EGG

CHICK

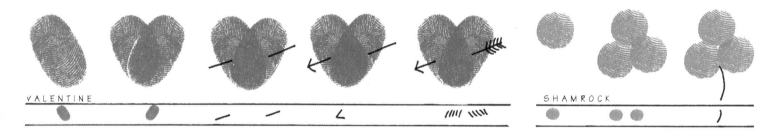

VALENTINE

SHAMROCK

LEPRECHAUN

30

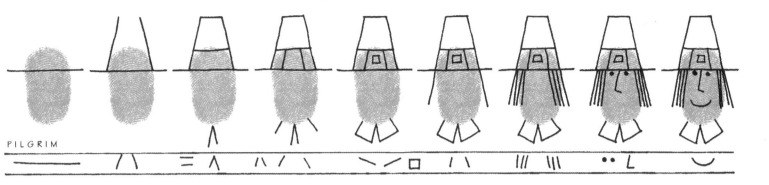

PILGRIM

TURKEY

PILGRIM

INDIAN

# HALLOWEEN

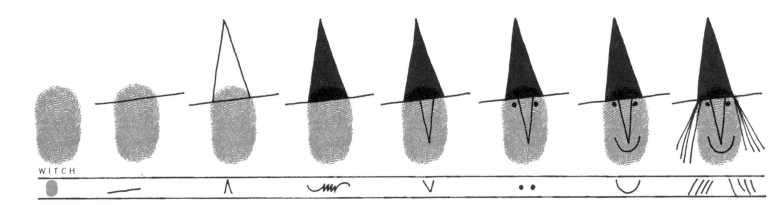

WITCH

BAT

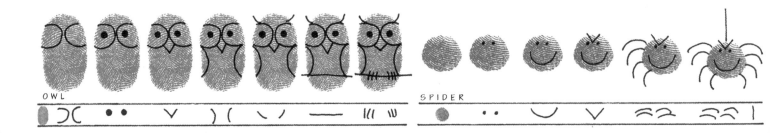

OWL

SPIDER

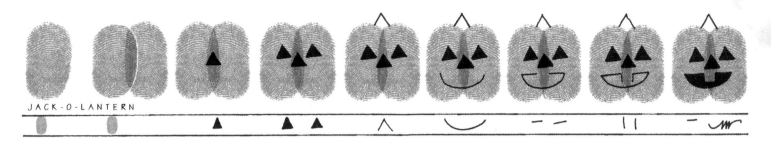

JACK-O-LANTERN

FLYING WITCH

SKELETON

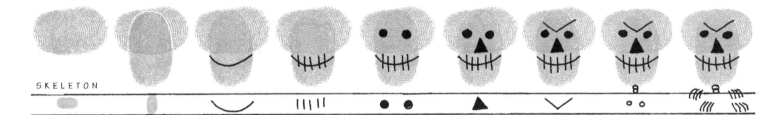

CAT

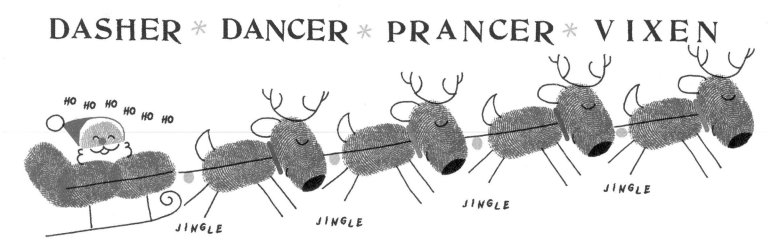

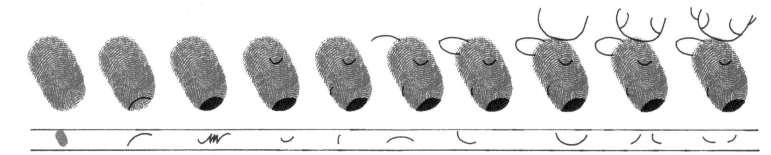

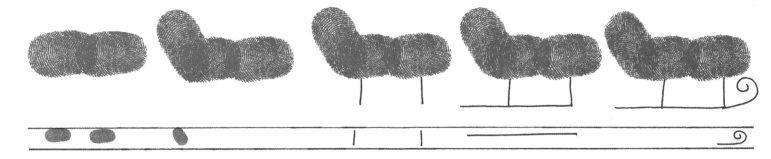

JINGLE  JINGLE  JINGLE

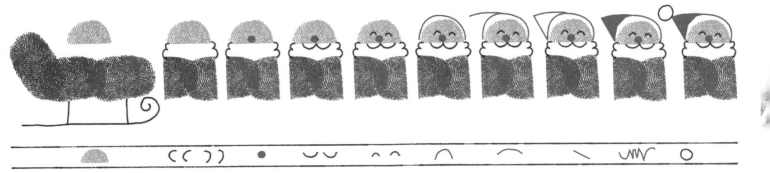

# LAND SEA AND AIR

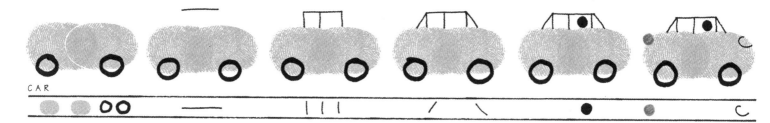

CAR

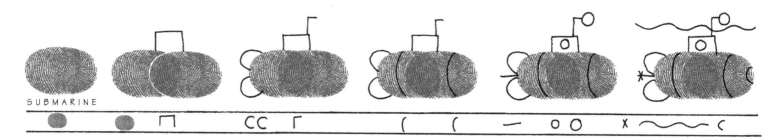

SUBMARINE

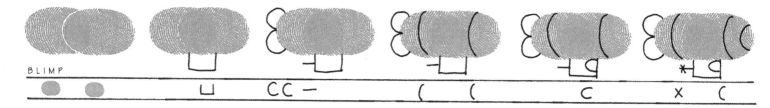

BLIMP

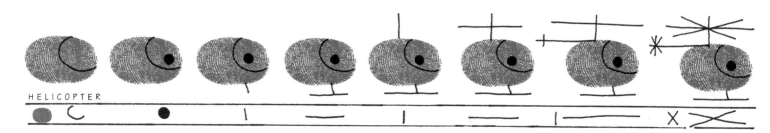

HELICOPTER

# TRAIN

ENGINE

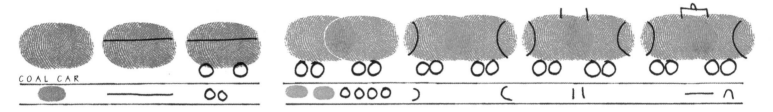

COAL CAR

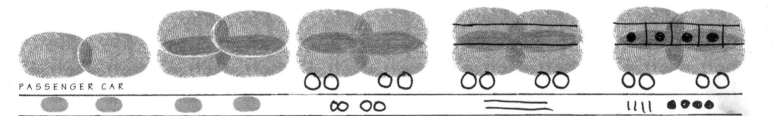

PASSENGER CAR

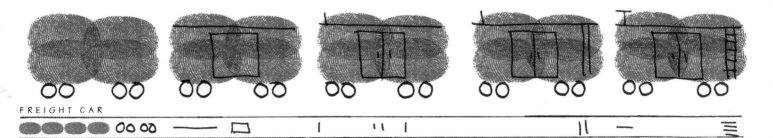

FREIGHT CAR

# RAINBOW CLOWN

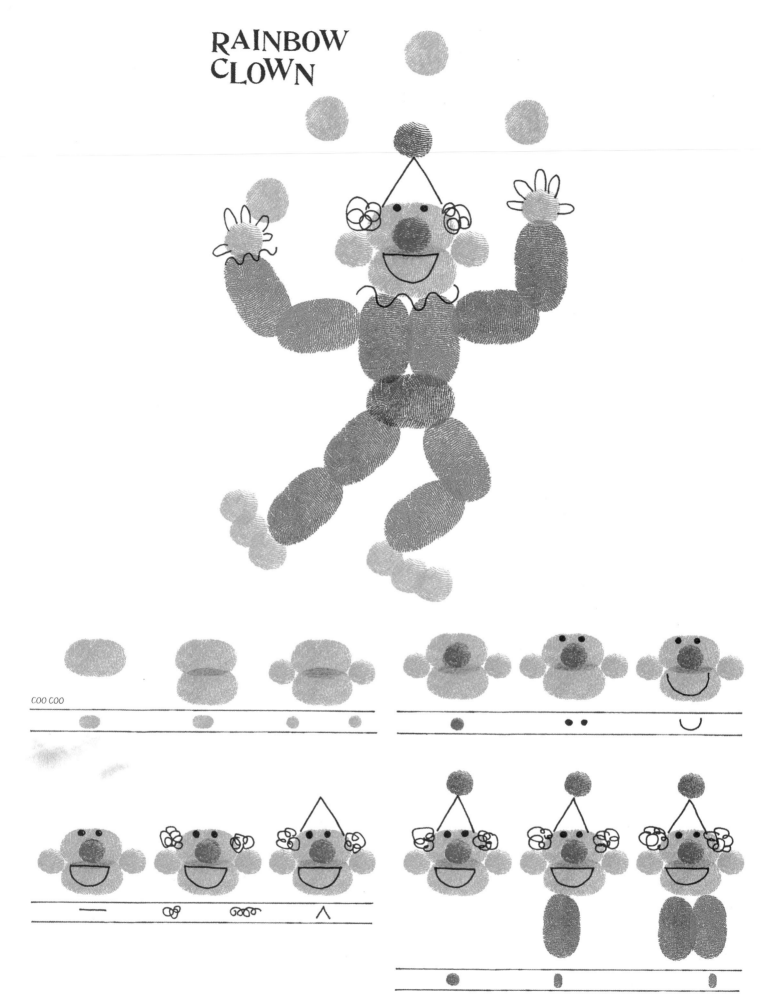

COO COO

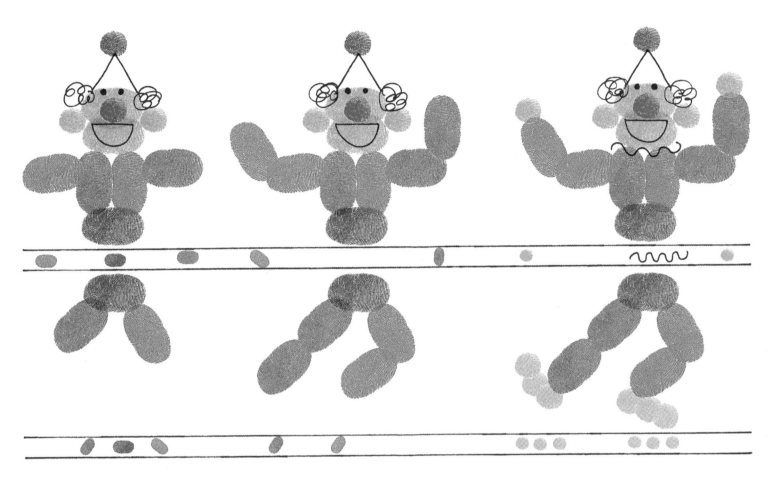

FESTER

LULU

# RAINBOW DRAGON

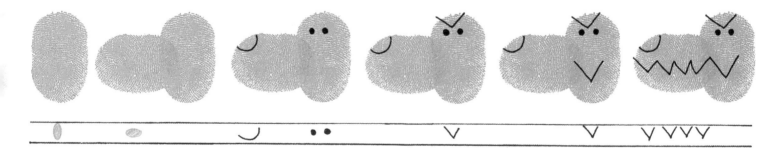

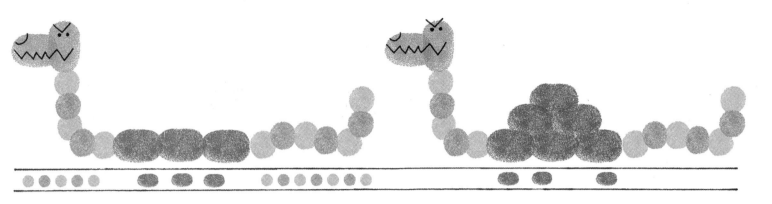

# LION

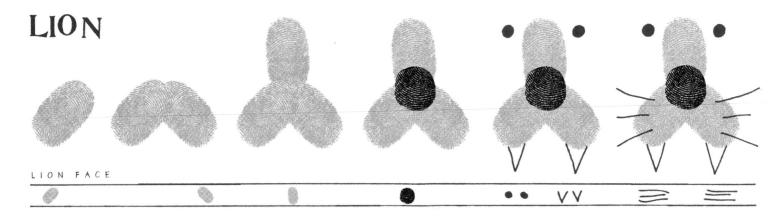

LION FACE

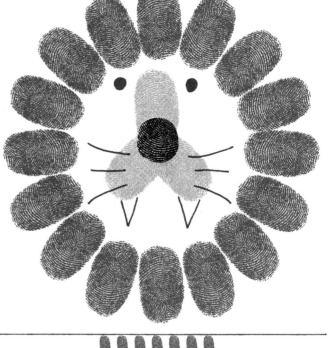

LION MANE

# RAINBOW
# LIONS

# SKETCH BOOK

HERE ARE SOME FINGERPRINT
THINGS I COULD NOT FIT INTO THIS
BOOK. CAN YOU FIGURE OUT HOW
I MADE THEM?

NOSES

HAIR

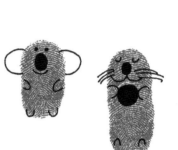 

EYES AND EARS

HATS

45

# ADVANCED FINGER-PRINTING

FOR THE ADVENTUROUS—
JUST A FEW OTHER WAYS TO COMBINE PRINTS,
COLORS, SIMPLE LINES, AND SOME
IMAGINATION TO MAKE PICTURES.
THERE ARE LOTS LEFT FOR YOU TO DISCOVER.
HAPPY DISCOVERING!

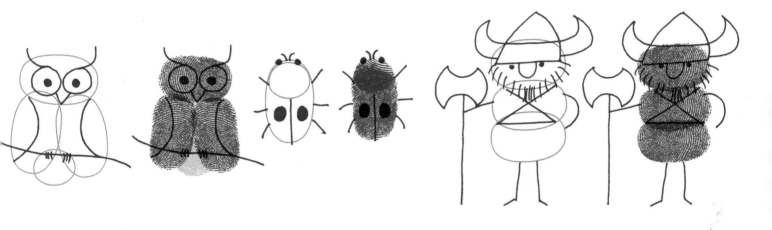

# SOMETHING VERY SPECIAL

The instructions in this book are meant to show a few ways to turn fingerprints into an owl or a cat or a dog, etc. Much has been left for you to explore and discover.

Just as no two fingerprints will ever look just alike, no two fingerprint pictures will ever look just alike. Fingerprints will be lighter or darker, lines will be thicker or thinner, colors will be different.

That means no other fingerprint pictures will look just like the ones in this book, or just like yours. That's what will make your pictures "something very special."

This is the way this book shows you how to make a fingerprint owl.

Here are some other "explorations."

Sometimes I like to use natural colors, sometimes I like to use imaginary colors.

Sometimes I like to use other fingerprints.

Sometimes I like to add a few extra lines.

Little, Brown and Company

Hachette Book Group

1290 Avenue of the Americas, New York, NY 10104

Visit our website at www.lb-kids.com

LB kids is an imprint of Little, Brown and Company. The LB kids name and logo are trademarks of Hachette Book Group, Inc.

First Revised Paperback Edition: June 2005

First published in hardcover in 1993 by Little, Brown and Company

Library of Congress Cataloging-in-Publication Data

Emberley, Ed.

[Fingerprint drawing book]

Ed Emberley's fingerprint drawing book—1st ed.

p. cm.

ISBN 978-0-316-78969-1

1. Fingerprints in art.   2. Drawing—Technique.   I. Title.

NC825.F55 E46 2001

741.2—dc21

00-031026

18 17 16 15 14 13

WKT

Printed in China